NOBODY

NOBODY

Alice Oswald

CAPE POETRY

3 5 7 9 10 8 6 4 2

Jonathan Cape, an imprint of Vintage,
20 Vauxhall Bridge Road,
London SW1V 2SA

Jonathan Cape is part of the Penguin Random House group
of companies whose addresses can be found at
global.penguinrandomhouse.com

Penguin
Random House
UK

First published by Jonathan Cape in 2019.
A collaboration with William Tillyer, incorporating
his watercolours, with an earlier text, was published in 2018.

penguin.co.uk/vintage

A CIP catalogue record for this book is available
from the British Library.

ISBN 9781787331969
Limited edition ISBN 9781787332126

Typeset by Kevin Mount, The Letter Press
Printed and bound in Great Britain by
TJ International Ltd, Padstow, Cornwall

Penguin Random House is committed to a sustainable future
for our business, our readers and our planet. This book is made
from Forest Stewardship Council® certified paper.

When Agamemnon went to Troy, he paid a poet to spy on his wife, but another man rowed the poet to a stony island and seduced her. Ten years later, Agamemnon came home and was murdered.

Odysseus, setting out at the same time, was blown off course. It took him another ten years to get home, but his wife, unlike Agamemnon's, had stayed faithful.

This poem lives in the murkiness between those stories. Its voice is wind-blown, water-damaged, as if someone set out to sing the Odyssey, but was rowed to a stony island and never discovered the poem's ending.

'Also there was a poet there, whom Agamemnon, when he went to Troy, ordered strictly to guard his wife; but once Fate had forced her to be seduced, then Aegistheus took the poet to a desert island and left him there as a lump of food for the birds, so the lover willingly took her willing to his house...'

(*The Odyssey* 3 267)

As the mind flutters in a man who has travelled widely
and his quick-winged eyes land everywhere
I wish I was there or there he thinks and his mind

immediately

as if passing its beam through cables
flashes through all that water and lands
less than a second later on the horizon
and someone with a telescope can see his tiny thought-form
floating on the sea-surface wondering what next

These stories flutter about
as fast as torchlight

even out here where the water is painfully clear
and to drown in it is to sense the movement of its colour
as a cold mathematical power have you not heard
even out here these stories
how in her house of silverware and deep baths
a woman began to dream she began to wake
and the heart stirring inside her clothes felt bruised
as if a hand was squeezing it

She said my friend someone is watching us you will not
win over you will not walk over me easily
as over the shallows of a river but Fate
that great failure of the will that great goddess
putting on a tremulous voice and smiling
and dressed in the white bathrobe of her lover
said dearest I have already doomed that watcher
I took him to an island the merest upthrust
of a stony shoulder sticking from the sea
and he paces there as dry as an ashtray
making up poems about us patchwork unfinished
while the sea-crows traipse to and fro regarding him sideways
what does it matter what he sings
there is all this water between us
and it is blind a kind of blind blue eye
it is alive it is dead it more or less ignores us
look at all these ripples everywhere complete with their shadows
I do not think a human for example
drowning in this measureless mosaic or floating up again
I do not think he will

hear us

These voices flit about quick-winged
with women's faces or land on a clifftop singing
so that here and there you find fading contrails of song
and a swimmer slooshing along breathing in and out
with the purple sea circling his throat always
thinks he can hear something which nevertheless escapes him

Poor man she says poor man it's obvious
the sea in its dark psychosis dreams of your death
but your upwardness your quick turnover like a wedge of polystyrene
always keeps you afloat this place is formless and unstable
it's as long as winter nevertheless you must swim
wind yourself in my veil and the sea which always senses your fear
will fall as flat as a pressed flower you shouldn't know this
it is not me but close to me a kind of cloud or smoke-ring
made of nothing and yet it will outlast everything
because it is deep it is a dead field fenceless
a thickness with many folds in it promiscuous and mingling
which in its patience always wears away the hard things

or is it only the hours on their rounds
thinking of the tides by turns
twelve white-collar workers
who manage the schedules of water
opening and shutting the mussel shells and adjusting
from black to turquoise the swinging sea-lights
so that the sun sinking through bladderwrack
into interminable aquarium
finds even far down there are white

stones

And suddenly in the violet dark
a bronze fish-hook flickers into life and out again

and when it rains and the sand has every ounce of me
marked at low tide and immediately forgotten
so that my footprints far into the future
go on sunkenly walking underneath me
when it rains it snows sometimes
as if falling asleep the body began to float

sideways

There are so many birds and most of them mean nothing
but once or twice a gannet
from a nest of slovenly seaweed
              hops
as far as those stones and stops
as a woman would remembering her son

but it is done madam nothing will close that wound
unless your shaken mind moving your pointed head
can stitch the water to the wind
or is it only her ghost going round and round
with a remnant of blue
and never a clue where to place it
or is it only that poet pacing to and fro
dreaming up rumours about the first kiss
buzzing on those lovers' flypaper lips

Small geometric figure
lost inside colour

he keeps wading out then back but it is
bottomless dusk down there pale black
nameless and numbness as when unfolding after sleeping
and your own dead foot has forgotten you
as if I waded inward
thirty yards from the surface of myself
but it's not myself it's just dark purple
it's not my feet it is the hours that move

if only the birds had subtitles if only by staring
I could draw some of those directions into my mind

And sometimes over my retina
as over an angled mirror an aeroplane
sometimes between two clouds with wingtips
teetering on the very pivot of vision a passenger
throws down her shadow
in which I catch the tiny movement of her eye-blinds

lifting

and in this cloud/uncloud I who can't settle
when I think of that crowd of colours on the sea
then my mind starts sliding towards them
borne on a wave of wind

As far as a man can shout across water
and his shout with blown-back wings
loses its bearings and is never heard of again
and another man can hear the crying waves
but his answer
dissolves in water like an oval of soap

they say this woman being twisted by sleep
began to hear things
as if the sea itself leaned over her bed
she could hear they say the exact note
in which a diver twizzles like a mobile
among triangular hanged fish
and the sea wall and the weakening cliffs
as far as the hem of her clothes

being eaten away

How does it start the sea has endless beginnings

About an hour ago she surfaced and shook her arms
and peered around and dived again and surfaced
and saw someone and dived again and surfaced
and smelt all those longings of grass-flower smells
and bird-flower sounds and the vaporous poems
that hang in the chills above rivers

With crooked elbows walking and small steps
she hops to these hollow limestone caves
where the seals breathing out the sea's bad breath
snuffle about all afternoon in sleeping bags
what kind of a rumour is beginning even now
under the waterlid she wonders there must be
hundreds of these broken and dropped-open mouths
sulking and full of silt on the seabed
I know a snorkeller found a bronze warrior once
with the oddest verdigris expression and maybe
even now a stranger is setting out
onto this disintegrating certainty this water
whatever it is whatever anything is
under these veils and veils of vision
which the light cuts but it remains

unbroken

So we floated out of sight into the unmarked air
and only our voices survived
like thistle-seed flying this way and that

a blue came over us a blue cloud
whose brown shadow goose-fleshed the sea
the ship after a little rush stopped moving
the wind with a swivelling sound began to rise
and here I am still divided in my decision
whether to heave-to or keep going under half-sail
but the water is in my thinking now
I remember the mast-pole broken by a gust
severed my two minds separate
and my body flopped like a diver over the side
then came the invisible then the visible rain
then icy and razor-sharp then green then dawn
who always wakes behind net curtains
and her watercolour character changes shade quickly like new leaves
she is excitable then shy then coppery pink
and raking her fingers around finds bits of clothing and bones

How strange she says among those better worlds underwater
where the cold of swimming is no different from the clear of looking
there are people still going about their work
unfurling sails and loosening knots
it's as if they didn't know they were drowned
it's as if I blinded by my own surface
have to keep moving over seemingly endless yellowness
have to keep moving over seemingly endless yellowness

How does the dawn trawler call out to the night trawler
when they pass each other on the black and white water

There are said to be microscopic insects in the eye
who speak Greek and these invisible
ambassadors of vision never see themselves
but fly at flat surfaces and back again
with pigment caught in their shivering hair-like receptors
and this is how the weather gets taken to and fro
and the waves pass each other from one colour to the next
and sometimes mist a kind of stupefied rain
slumps over the water like a teenager
and sometimes the sun returns whose gold death mask
with its metallic stare seems to be

blinking

Two fishermen rowing across saw something jagged and disturbing
the long-drawn-out Now of a teenager
pale green and full of unripe hope
he had dressed himself in wings this is exciting
I like the angle of attack when these graded feathers
glued in their waxy grooves begin to swim the air

winding his giddiness up and up
carrying his steadfast sceptical stare
right to the summit of sight he noticed suddenly
his fate had been found out and flapping his arms

flushed

and almost glad to give up

he began to

fall

What a relief to hear his flesh
with hair and clothes flaring backwards like a last-minute flower
hit the sea and finally understand itself
his human-salt already at ease in the ocean-salt
and the white silt-like substance of exhaustion
blending with the water

        if only

if only my eyes could sink under the surface
and join those mackerel shoals in their matching suits
whose shivering inner selves all inter-mirrored
all in agreement with water
wear the same

wings

But this is the sea
still with its back to me
in its flesh of a thousand faces all facing away
and who can decipher this
voice among voices

     listen

This is one kind of water when it hangs over him
a man is a nobody underneath a big wave
his loneliness expands his hair floats out like seaweed
and when he surfaces his head full of green water
sitting alone on his raft in the middle of death
then it is wide it is a wide field of horrible upheavals
there are fish in it there are shearwaters searching
and sometimes in these gulfs a goddess
who used to be human now she is yellow-eyed
sometimes she shrieks heavy-winged with laughterless laughter
and lands on his raft shaking the underworld off
poor man she says poor man it's obvious
you can sniff it everywhere the shabby weirdness
of the sea-god leaning intimately over
and turning his shadows against you
poor morsel of cork you bob about
throwaway in all this what is it grief grief grief
but this grief is so old its matter has lost its mind
blinks blinks and sees nothing
howls howls and hears nothing

And yet again water still in acute discomfort

always yearning and hallucinating and dedicated to the wind
and yet again the wind not fully awake
or was it laughter blew me along I lost track of
the underneath of things everything became my mirror
once I stood up to look over the side
I sat down again terrified it was myself I saw
thronged and pitch-green
spilling over the lip of the earth
the same soft dust-sheets over my hands as the clouds
the same thick curtain across the horizon as
sheer boredom and a deep

      sea-breath

In which a spirit leaning languorously from a porthole
poured stillness over the sea like a jug of milk
and there were bones everywhere and feathered people
stood singing on the stones on rickety thin legs
with tilted chins and pressed flat wings

If you should see they said if you could spare
a moment to make out if you have any heart
to hear us mourn in short syllables
now that the stillness is pale blue
and apparitions of islands like pre-world humans
are waiting to evolve but always before they can grow detail
the air aborts them and the clouds
bafflingly quiet as if the fact of floating
had taken some weight off their minds
the clouds pause like holy men
very close and far-off in their white shrouds of office

If you should see a pair of blinking eyes
blue and red with weeping no sooner seen than gone
you should know they are kingfishers
man and wife in these amazing clothes
who lay their eggs on fish-bones
and for nine days when they nest the wind drops
and the hooded waves remembering their story
stammer to a hush they used to be humans

whose flesh stalks always true to the light
were on the point of flowering but the sea
which has no faith no patience
just kleptomaniac and fickle currents

drowned him

It was horrible when the rising sun
wrinkled her skin as it worked its way in
and the widow at the window saw at once
her bloated husband's head oh pray for the crowded
ragged dead in the crypts of the sea
where the boneless octopus
                    only exists by endlessly altering
pray for the hollowed out souls
in the skins of the living whose lifted clothes

                became

                    birds

When trees take over an island and say so all at once
some in pigeon some in pollen with a coniferous hiss
and run to the shore shouting for more light
and the sun drops its soft coverlet over their heads
and owls and hawks and long-beaked sea-crows
flash to and fro
like spirits of sight whose work is on the water
where the massless mind undulates the intervening air
shading it blue and thinking

        I wish I was there

or there

A goddess or fog-shape in full wedding dress
sulks in that loneliness what a winter creature
whose lover loathes the everlasting clouds of her
and sits in tears staring at the pleasure-crinkled sea
but she as if a dash of hope
discoloured her sight stands waiting
the way a spider when it wishes to travel
simply lets out a silken

      aerial

electrostatically alert through every hair
to the least shift of the ionosphere
at last it lifts on tiptoe and lovely to behold
like a bare twig it begins to blow
wherever the wind will take it but the wind
is the most distracted messenger I know

Whereupon the water turned in its cloak
and shook itself into flames and burnt itself into fur
and tore itself into flesh and told everything
and instantly shrank into polythene
and withered and bloomed and resolved to be less faltering

                    and failed

and became a jellyfish a mere weakness of water
a morsel of ice a glamour of oil
and became a fish-smell and then a rotting seal
and then an old mottled man full of mood-swings
forgetting his name and twisting his hands
denying and distorting and thinking ill of everything
he snapped himself into sticks and burst into leaves
which fell back down again as water
blue-green and black-shine with white lining
and blinked himself into thousands of self-seeing eyes
like a piece of writhing paper in five seconds of fire
destroying its light with its

light

And so the sun brought measurement to everything
all but the sea frightened of its own stupidity
and on every cliffside luminous lilies
made their escape through stones
whose swinging stems
were merely the lowest ruffling hems of the passing of spring
and above them flying in verse

in time with
the wind

Two sisters in shock
one couldn't speak one couldn't stop
she knocked on the bedroom window

sister
        hello

what with tutting and whistling
she shoved her way in through the door
well sister if they cut out your tongue
you'll have to thread this needle and stitch me the facts
and as she stitched and stitched those sordid facts
broke through her feathered smile and became a beak

As when the moon shines through tent walls
making black-and-white films of the woods
so that the sleepers seem to float through trees
so those two sisters
out through their back-lit flesh they fly
into the blue of amnesia

snapping at insects and can't think why

Terrified of insects of noon of sunlight
when the sea dilates to let more green in
and the damaged undermost in all its clefts can be seen
when swallows free themselves of their sorrows
and seagulls hang themselves on invisible armatures
and only a few tiny almost magical flashes of light
fall in the form of rain and

stop

those lovers lurk in their indoors wondering
can he hear us now that poet has he finished
his poem about us what kind of a sting in the ending
will he sing of the husband if he is in fact
on his way here knowing by now the craggy out-jut
of that shallow place where the seals bob about like footballs
and did you hear along the shore that chorus of trees
with seaweed hung from their twigs like wept-in tissue
being moved by what a heartfelt sigh the wind is
and have you noticed the way the radius of water
maintains itself in proportion to its circles
as if each raindrip made a momentary calculation
and when it stops there are ruled flat lines
running from one island metrically to another

How does it start the sea has endless beginnings

There is a harbour where an old sea-god sometimes surfaces
two cliffs keep out the wind you need no anchor
the water in fascinated horror holds your boat
at the far end a thin-leaved olive casts a kind of evening over a cave
which is water's house where it leads its double life
there are four stone bowls and four stone jars
and the bees of their own accord leave honey there
salt-shapes hang from the roof like giant looms
where the tide weaves leathery sea-nets
be amazed by that colour it is the mind's inmost madness
but the sea itself has no character just this horrible thirst
goes on creeping over the stones and shrinking away

The sea she said and who could ever drain it dry
has so much purple in its caves the wind at dusk
incriminates the waves
and certain fish conceal it in their shells
at ear-pressure depth
where the shimmer of headache dwells
and the brain goes

     dark
         purple

           who could offend the sea there is so much water
we might as well waste this ever-replenished
fairy-tale stuff don't flinch she said
I want you to walk this carpet

        please oh please

you must be so so
footsore after your ten-year war you surely
deserve a little something if you
take off your shoes the bare floor will be so cold so
filthily infectious you should step down safely

here

That man is doomed that very second
the swelling blood-shade shows through his skin
even as he bashfully sets his foot down saying
after all I'm not nobody maybe I deserve a little
brighter something than my allotted brightness
no superstition has ever hurt an honest man perhaps
after my bath in my towel I can walk it

again

Inside his lifted foot in its falling pause
Fate feeds on this weakness and the same
massive simplicity cuts through his throat
as drips and sways in all these

      tide

         filled

         caves

the same iridescent swiftness and the same
uncertain certainty either brimming or rippled
or swelling over of hollowing water
as one thought leads to another if you stand
here on these boulders with your back to the earth
you can see the whole story of the weather
the way the wind brings one shadow after another
but another one always sweeps up behind
and no-one can decipher this lucid short-lived
chorus of waves it is too odd and even
as if trying to remember some perfect prehistoric
pattern of spirals it is too factual too counter-factual
too copper-blue too irregular-metrical

listen

Let me tell you what the sea does
to those who live by it first it shrinks then it
hardens and simplifies and half-buries us
and sometimes you find us shivering in museums
with tilted feet so that all we can do is lie flat
our colourful suffering faces watered away
we who threw fish-lines into these waves
and steadied our weight in mastless longboats
and breathed in and out the very winds that wrecked us

And there are herons there are sea-ravens
whose wingspan is a whole awning
they could lift a man's flesh off its framework
and cormorants like eroded crows
and angled ospreys and harpies
all kinds of long-beaked hungers
peer from the trees and any minute now
with smashing of wings and probing of steel-grey pins
they'll come for these eyes oh horrible

      flightless

  light

I've always loved the way when night happens
the blood is drawn off is sucked and soaked upwards
out of the cliff-flowers the way they worn out
surrender their colours and close and then the sky
suffers their insights all the shades of mauve green blue
move edgelessly from west to east the cold
comes ghostly out of holes and the earth it's strange
as soon as she shuts her sky-lids her hindsights open
and you can see right out through her blindness
as far as the ancient stars still making their precise points
still exactly visible and then not exactly

well there was and there was not a drowned woman
still visible underwater crossing a field
there she walks nothing can shift that moment
lodged in her chest when she was kidnapped
and her outline stayed there forever but she
now with no character only this salty bitterness
became a slave she who had rich parents
began to smell of anger sinking towards unendurable laughter
which overruns its circle like the sea itself
on whose blind glare
a boat appears full of rat-eyed sailors
squinting from watching too much sea-film

Image after image it never ends
it has the texture of plough but with no harvest
but every so often a flower of light floats past
and one of them slept with her which is a woman's weakness
we must keep it she said hidden under eyelids
put lampshades on this eagerness if we meet
at the fountain for example washing our clothes or drinking
but after a while he grew bored of this patience
he came to her door with necklaces
she had a needle in her hand she looked up sharp
and her mind slipped like snow off a leaf
but the gods know everything they sent a virus
fluttering after the ship and seven days later
she dropped like a dead bird into the bilge
four sailors had to swing her over the side and the water
with all its claws and eaters closed over her
the splash became a series of dots and
under that sound the green sea turned

        grey

Transparent wisps of things with eye-like organs
sink to the seabed in shells of extraordinary beauty
and at sunset the smells float out orange
and settle on the flowers' tongues while sea-whips
thrash thrash the water for a living
nobody cares whether there is weeping or oozing
or the flavour of dead flesh fills the evening
and when the wind shifts you can hear a man
shouting for help
   cursing his wounded foot but
   nobody answers

Only night-birds eating insects
whirring and dialling in the small hours
expressing no emotion only existence
always laughing and screaming the same fact
stacked on every twig not every sound
is a voice not every breath is a self
but anything
knocked by a sudden blow
has the same unspecified shrillness oh I
feel like a glued fly giving up and standing up and
time and again stuck in the same pain if only
my foot could move my thought
and think of a cure but my thoughts can't
lift their wings and every struggle
tangles me lower I wish I was

there or

there

Misfortune I wish I could meet you
underwater in your deep green room
and flannel your bloodshot eyes
and brush your dead hair
they say there is a flash of mercy
concealed in your face-folds
if only a person has time to swim down
and find it

there are soft chairs no windows
no noise except the self-closing stone door
which I opened once
and found myself in a chamber of options
a little sea-cleft where the salmon drift
and turn into humans

but Fate is not Fortune
I was not fated to find you there
only the converging walls

        the tilted
        floor

And once a fisherman poking among the mackerel
pulled out a human head whose head
tell me muse about this floating nobody
the one who would have drowned but a river
coming looking for him with swerves
and trailing beard-hair how secretive it is
when water moves through the sea
keeping its muddiness intact and fish commuters
hurry under him as if motioning him in
this river touched his hand who is it
honourable river-god is it you he said
o cold tap cold mouth pick up this message o help me
I come to you upside-down with empty suckers
crawling along the sea surface on my knees
stripped of everything even gravity have mercy

Tell me muse about this ancient passer-by
who found himself adrift in infinite space
with all the planets flying in loops around him
like listless gods
all kinds of light and unlight he witnessed
until his eye-metal rusted away
and now there is no going back no edge no law
no horizon or harbour-wall or rubble breakwater
can keep out this formless from his sightless
nevertheless the grey sea-voice lapping at his skull
even through closed teeth goes on whispering

There was once a stubborn man
searching the earth for the guillemot that speaks
who came at last to the breakneck cliffs and paused
a sleek bird studied him as if to say
you must be that southerner
fated to die of fright if I speak
and a woman once let go of her posture
and shoved herself in a barrel onto the waves
it felt so right to feel her thoughts
hitting her skull

       one person has the character of dust
another has an arrow for a soul
but their stories all end

       somewhere

         in the sea

Then we went down to the sea to our black boat
first we dragged the boat into the lively water
and set up mast and sails and drove the sheep on board
then climbed in ourselves depressed crying lukewarm tears
and our hostess who is a goddess long-haired inhuman
but her language is human except when she sings
those bitter grief-songs sent a fair wind
like a friend following a few steps behind
and we busied about securing the ship's tackle
and sat in our places while the wind and the pilot steered us out
all that day the sails at full-stretch drew us over the water
until the sun sank and the roads let slip their shadows
then our boat reached the outer edge of the sea
that feeling of water in its own world moving underneath us
where the blind people live lost under a cloth of fog
and the sun can never burn through it to find them
not when it floats up into space
not when it turns and sinks into the earth
but night always stretches a dark membrane over those people

And there I saw the crumpled criminal face of someone
in the fog of her body not knowing what she did
she murdered her husband obscene night
first the gods found out then everyone else
but she her whole soul strangled with horrors
knelt in the bathroom scrubbing and scrubbing
the green of her husband's and her daughter's
disfigured corpse-forms and thought-storms
being lifted up and down as dazed as plankton
it's fine she thought as long as I keep smiling
not mentioning the blood on my nails then nothing
will pass my weakness out between these pointed teeth-posts
not even the murdered one with his last breath
not even necessity will sniff me out

or will she

Purpled mind
why go on circling

There is a channel where an old sea-god swims
on translucent wings
five miles down in deep unflowered
midnight where it snows and heaps up salt
this goblin-god with ghost-grace frictionlessly
moves
or hangs like a pickled heart in the sea-jar

nothing I say sinks down that far

worn-out god can you hear this
look up please from the interstellar hangings
of your under-the-horizon house
there is blood on the tiles
the husband has died struck by his own wife
as he stood naked in the bath

can you hear this

No

not

me

A tired man clinging to a stony out-jut
after a three-hour storm after a ten-year war
clinging to that final handhold thinking
god can you hear this

no

        not

                me

there he sways under the switched-off swinging bulb of the moon
his ship has gone and he is the last man
lashed to the last upright in the roaringnothing thinking
now I really am somebody women are going to love
this quirk I have of outlasting war cloud sickness everything
even water ha! little does he know
what a willpower even now at a hundred miles an hour
is rushing towards his boast with the same wide-open mouth
ready to out-character him and fill his gaping laughter
with salt water now that his handhold
breaks away in his hands and his head drops into the sea

Why is my mind this untranslatable colour of scratchiness and indecision
as of twilight turning into a night accused of corpses
my answer is a swift one a goddess a hundred-mile-an-hour readiness
flying alongside me and I ask you
who would willingly travel over so much water
like a permanent rain-cloud crizzling the sea
so that the waves grow nervous covering up their crimes
but truth will always out and so will

falsehood

That goddess pierced by clear-sightedness
falling out of the air as winged and sudden as luck
        like flicking a light-switch
                    flash
in the dark of these words she stood here
just a minute ago dead but alive in man's clothes saying
stranger weeping without stopping
cutting off the conversations of those who have a right to be frivolous
it is human to have a name but you seem unsolid somehow
almost too porous to be human I would say
some terrible repetition has eaten into you
as water eats into metal this is what happens
whenever love is mentioned your whole heart liquefies
and the character of water stares out through your eyes
it's as if you were a woman maybe her mind wanders
but it's clear her flesh is damaged in some way
as she drops to her knees and cries and so begins
the simple mineral monologue of

water

Who is it saying these things is it only the tide
passing like a rumour over the sea-floor or
who is it keeps silent
when somebody's ring on nobody's hand
sinks like an eye into darkness
and the wind drops
and the water roars itself speechless

who is it speaking she said
my friend
who is it watching me behind your eyelids

Please he said will you please let me sleep

fidgeting under his quilt with one foot touching the floor
you know full well he said this is only the water
talking to us in the voice of amnesia
sometimes with scraping anxious steps
turning over the stones and sometimes
howling the same question over and over
and on his rock that poet shuffles about light-sleeping
every so often answering back

who is it

but for all this for maybe a thousand years
it's been the same answer to the same question

no-one

and on the roof the caretaker scarcely blinks
staring at the sea-sky wondering which way up
he is nailed to the night in case your husband
dressed in his fate but as yet

unmurdered

suddenly appears

But for all this for maybe a thousand years
it's been the same answer to the same question

nothing

Into which a star a whole unsynchronised solar system
throwing out light like a splash of yellow paint across the night
or else a burning angel falling out of heaven
with briefcase open and his charred documents
drifting about his head descending
from floor to floor he looks liquefied
like a towering sea-plume and finally his feet
which seem to have no difficulty with water
touch down on the horizon without friction

as a seagull sleighs down waves
and wets its stiff wings in the horrible sea-hollows
looking for fish so he swerves and stalls
and finds a woman sitting very still and cold
and wizened with permanent headache on her island
one hand like the shadow of an aeroplane
barely moving over her own blue surface
waves him away she says I know

I know

and the little breezes of her speeches smell like parsley

You are a messenger and you've come to remove my lover
who is tired of this hotel life you'll find him
sitting on the dunes in tears as always
staring at the sea's round eye of course
Fate has its needle in him nothing can stop him draining away
there seem to be two worlds one is water's
which always finds its level one is love's which doesn't
but is wide a wide field of horrible upheavals
there are gleams mists gusts is he hoping to float himself
on that never-ending to and fro
where the mind no longer belongs to the mind
and a man's shout boomerangs in the wind
the light has no ceiling there are human hands
stuck in the sand like kelp-stalks
and huge cathedrals of waves

a single

moth

struggles under wet sails
but everything warm or weighted always

falls

So she shrieks and flies up laughing and loud-speakering
and turns and dives unable to be anything for long
and the black wave covers her

C L Y T E M N E S T R A A E G I S T H E U S N
D M U S M E L I C E R T E S E I D O T H E A P
E L I O S N O B O D Y I C A R O S L I G E A A
C Y O N E C A L Y P S O A G A M E M N O N P
M O N B A U C I S P H O E N I S S A P H I L O
O R P H E U S N O B O D Y C I R C E L E U C
P E H E L I O S A J A X A T H E N E A N D R O
Y N O B O D Y C L Y T E M N E S T R A A E G
O T H E A C A D M U S M E L I C E R T E S E
O S E I D O N H E L I O S N O B O D Y I C A R
I A C E Y X A L C Y O N E C A L Y P S O A G A
E U S P H I L E M O N B A U C I S P H O E N I
M N E S T R A O R P H E U S N O B O D Y C I
S P E N E L O P E H E L I O S A J A X A T H E

```
 D Y ODYSSEUS L E U C O T H E A C A
 C Y S E O S A L C Y O N E P O S E I D O N H
 S T H E U S T H E L X I E P E I A C E Y X A L
 N E P H I L O M E L P R O T E U S P H I L E
 T E S C A L Y P S O C L Y T E M N E S T R A
 E A O R E S T E S G L A U K O S P E N E L O
 H E H E R M E S P O S E I D O N N O B O D
 I E U S N O B O D Y O D Y S S E U S L E U C
 T H E A P H O R C Y S E O S A L C Y O N E P
 I G E A AEGISTHEUS T H E L X I E P E
 N O N P R O C N E P H I L O M E L P R O T
 P H I L O C T E T E S C A L Y P S O C L Y T E
 L E U C O T H E A O R E S T E S G L A U K O
 N D R O M A C H E H E R M E S P O S E I D O
```

C L Y T E M N E S T R A **A E G I S T H E U S** N
D M U S M E L I C E R T E S E I D O T H E A P
E L I O S N O B O D Y I C A R O S L I G E A
C Y O N E **C A L Y P S O** A G A M E M N O N P
M O N B A U C I S P H O E N I S S A P H I L O
O R P H E U S N O B O D Y **C I R C E** L E U C
P E H E L I O S A J A X A T H E N E A N D R O
Y N O B O D Y C L Y T E M N E S T R A A E G
O T H E A C A D M U S M E L I C E R T E S E
O S E I D O N H E L I O S N O B O D Y I C A R
I A C E Y X A L C Y O N E C A L Y P S O A G A
E U S P H I L E M O N B A U C I S P H O E N I
M N E S T R A **O R P H E U S** N O B O D Y C I
S P E N E L O P E H E L I O S A J A X A T H E

```
D Y O D Y S S E U S L E U C O T H E A C A
C Y S E O S A L C Y O N E P O S E I D O N H
S T H E U S T H E L X I E P E I A C E Y X A L
N E P H I L O M E L P R O T E U S P H I L E
T E S C A L Y P S O C L Y T E M N E S T R A
E A O R E S T E S G L A U K O S P E N E L O
H E H E R M E S P O S E I D O N N O B O D
E U S N O B O D Y O D Y S S E U S L E U C
H E A P H O R C Y S E O S A L C Y O N E P
I G E A A E G I S T H E U S T H E L X I E P E
N O N P R O C N E P H I L O M E L P R O T
H I L O C T E T E S C A L Y P S O C L Y T E
L E U C O T H E A O R E S T E S G L A U K O
N D R O M A C H E H E R M E S P O S E I D O
```

C L Y T E M N E S T R A A E G I S T H E U S I

D M U S M E L I C E R T E S E I D O T H E A I

E L I O S **NOBODY** I C A R O S L I G E A

C Y O N E C A L Y P S O A G A M E M N O N P

M O N B A U C I S P H O E N I S S A P H I L O

O R P H E U S **NOBODY** C I R C E L E U C

P E H E L I O S A J A X A T H E N E A N D R O

Y **NOBODY** C L Y T E M N E S T R A A E G

O T H E A C A D M U S M E L I C E R T E S E

O S E I D O N H E L I O S **NOBODY** I C A

I A C E Y X A L C Y O N E **CALYPSO** A G A

E U S P H I L E M O N B A U C I S P H O E N I

M N E S T R A O R P H E U S **NOBODY** C

S P E N E L O P E H E L I O S A J A X A T H E

```
ODYODYSSEUSLEUCOTHEACA
CYSEOSALCYONEPOSEIDONH
STHEUSTHELXIEPEIACEYXAL
NEPHILOMELPROTEUSPHILE
TESCALYPSOCLYTEMNESTRA
EAORESTESGLAUKOSPENELO
HEHERMESPOSEIDONNOBOD
EUS NOBODY ODYSSEUSLEUC
THEAPHORCYSEOSALCYONEP
IGEAAEGISTHEUSTHELXIEPE
NONPROCNEPHILOMELPROT
PHILOCTETESCALYPSOCLYTE
LEUCOTHEAORESTESGLAUKO
NDROMACHEHERMESPOSEIDO
```

NOBODY was commissioned by Bernard Jacobson
to accompany the watercolours of William Tillyer
and was first published by 21 Publishing in 2018 as
an art book, edited by Paul Keegan and typeset by
Kevin Mount. The poem is designed to be mobile
and so it has been rewritten for Jonathan Cape,
edited by Robin Robertson and reset by Kevin
Mount. I am very grateful to all those mentioned
and also to Anna Webber and Seren Adams.